Plante Moran
Detroit Team —

Welcome to Detroit!

Your Friends at
Clark Hill Detroit
Yai

The Way It Was

Published by Momentum Books, L.L.C., a subsidiary of HOUR Media, L.L.C.

117 West Third Street
Royal Oak, Michigan 48067
www.momentumbooks.com

FIRST EDITION: December 2004

ISBN 1-879094-71-1
LCCN 2004112963

The Way It Was

GLIMPSES OF DETROIT'S HISTORY
FROM THE PAGES OF *HOUR DETROIT* MAGAZINE

MOMENTUM BOOKS, L.L.C.
ROYAL OAK, MICHIGAN

CONTRIBUTING WRITERS:
GEORGE BULANDA, RICHARD BAK, MICHELLE CIAVOLA

Introduction

IF, AS IT HAS BEEN SUGGESTED, THAT PHOTOGRAPHS PROVIDE THE SOCIAL FOOTSTEPS OF TIME, THEN the book you hold in your hands is a veritable walking tour through Detroit's history.

These footprints are inextinguishable, permanent records of a time and place that say: This happened, these people existed, this building once stood. The photos in this volume were culled from the back pages of *HOUR Detroit* magazine, offering a representative glimpse back at the way Detroit was, from the earliest shot, 1880, to the most recent, 1987. The Way It Was is a popular feature with the magazine's readers, many of whom begin reading each issue from the back page first. Some readers recall events or buildings because they lived through that particular time. Youthful readers, familiar only with a largely forlorn city, are frequently astounded by images of a town that was once pulsating with energy and crowds.

Most of these pictures don't depict important or cataclysmic moments in the city's history, although there certainly are shots of famous people visiting Detroit, from John F. Kennedy speaking to a downtown crowd, to Eleanor Roosevelt officiating at a slum clearance, to Frank Sinatra performing at Cobo Hall, to Louis Armstrong blasting his trumpet at a country club. But the majority are simply images capturing a time and place that are no more. In their spontaneity, they evoke life as it was lived.

Archival photographs are easy enough to come by, but it can be challenging to find an image that also tells a story. A photo of a theater's exterior is only mildly interesting. But add a cluster of people in front of that building, queuing up in anticipation of viewing a blockbuster film, and that photograph suddenly possesses vitality. You're able to see people's facial expressions, the strange fashions of the day, the quaint old automobiles and so on.

HOUR *Detroit* strives to publish images that suggest a story or evoke an era, regardless of the year. It's purely coincidental, for instance, that there are more photos in this book from 1910 and 1954 than any other years.

The past can be deceptive. Some folks burrow into it to find comfort or illusion. There's a temptation to view everything as a golden age, when neighborhoods were safe, when people were kinder and friend-lier, when everything was simpler. Sometimes we don't want to face the melancholy fact that things will never, can never, be the same. The downtown Hudson's may conjure up a flood of fond memories, but the reality is that it's gone for good, collapsed by a powerful implosion in October of 1998. Yesterday, when com-pared with the turbulence and uncertainty of today or tomorrow, is consoling. There's a warm familiarity about the past we find reassuring.

There's some truth in all that. But history, of course, has its bleak, ugly moments. We tend to forget that the Great Depression hit Detroit especially hard, when industrious men lost their jobs, and families were evicted from their homes. And although World War II helped galvanize Detroiters into building the Arsenal of Democracy, people lived fearfully of madmen in distant places — and the agony that they could receive at any time the piercingly sorrowful telegram that a loved one had died fighting in Europe or in the

Pacific. And even the greenest student of our city's history can't gloss over the fact that two riots — in 1943 and 1967 — tore Detroit apart.

And while we look back fondly at, say, women in white gloves enjoying lunch at a downtown hotel, there's the grim and often ignored fact that an entire segment of society — merely because of their skin color — often couldn't gain entry to certain hotels, restaurants and retailers.

Still, the past for many was indeed rosy, brimming with happy memories of good times and good people. Sometimes, the "good old days" really *were* good.

"It is what it is" is an oft-heard remark today, implying that you can't change the essential character of something. "It was what it was" seems an apt description of Detroit's past. We can neither erase nor change it. How we remember it is up to us, although after looking at these 72 images, I suspect most readers will be stirred by sweet memories, tender sentiment and even yearning.

So enjoy this journey on Detroit's time machine. Just remember the road back to the here and now.

George Bulanda, Managing Editor
HOUR Detroit magazine

1880

FOR THOSE WITH A WEAKNESS FOR DESSERTS, THE NAME SANDERS CONJURES up the sweetest memories. In 1875, Fred Sanders opened a small confectionery in downtown Detroit at Woodward and Gratiot, which blossomed into the "Pavilion of Sweets" at Woodward and Michigan (seen here). Soon every metro Detroit neighborhood had a Sanders retail store and soda fountain. Scores of Detroiters succumbed to the allures of Sanders bumpy chocolate cake, caramel or hot fudge sundaes, lemon sodas, hot fudge cream puffs or Boston coolers, as well as light lunches and soups served by waitresses in pink uniforms. After a trip to the lunch counter, it was impossible to resist the displays of candy and baked goods for sale. Visitors to Sanders always left a little heavier but a lot happier. Sanders stores all are closed now, but the company's toppings, candy and baked goods still are available at supermarkets and other retailers.

—∞∞∞—

1885

There are few remnants of the 19th century left standing in Detroit, but Historic Fort Wayne is one of the rare places where the atmosphere and architecture of the 1800s remain intact. Built in 1845 during a tense period with the British, Fort Wayne was erected as a citadel against invasion from Canada. Despite its military associations, the grounds of the 83-acre site have always been tranquil. "There never has been a shot fired in anger at Fort Wayne," says Bob Sadler, director of marketing and communications for the Detroit Historical Museums. Once the threat vanished, Fort Wayne, located at West Jefferson and Livernois in southwest Detroit, turned into an Army training and induction center, from the Civil War to the Vietnam conflict. During World War II, the fort also served as a parts depot. "Fort Wayne was at the center of action when Detroit became the Arsenal of Democracy," Sadler says. The fort also housed Italian POWs during World War II, as well as displaced people burned out of their homes during the 1967 riot. This photo shows soldiers conferring in the foreground. In the rear are homes where families of officers lived. Fort Wayne closed to the public in 1992, and many of the crumbling buildings further deteriorated. But gradually, Fort Wayne (or Historic Fort Wayne, as it's come to be known) is being renovated. It's once again open to the public on weekends between Memorial Day and Labor Day, with guided tours and Civil War re-enactments among the attractions.

1889

ALTHOUGH PROFESSIONAL SPORTS WERE BEGINNING TO GAIN A TOEHOLD in Detroit, amateur athletes still dominated the local sporting scene. Standing in the doorway of the original Detroit Athletic Club at Woodward and Forest, sporting a derby, is John C. Lodge, who like most of his fellow club members played cricket interchangeably with baseball. The longtime city council member, who started his political career in 1897, obviously learned a little about pinch-hitting, as he twice filled in for resigning mayors in the 1920s before serving a full term himself. Like many others who came of age during the era of amateur competition, Lodge had little regard for the professional athletes of the 20th century. In his old age he professed that he never "had the chance" to watch Hall of Famer Charlie Gehringer play during his two decades with the Detroit Tigers — a startling but revealing admission for someone who lived and worked his entire life within walking distance of Michigan and Trumbull. Lodge retired from the city council in 1948 at age 85 and died two years later. The John C. Lodge Freeway is named for him, though Lodge, true to his horse-and-buggy roots, never learned how to drive a car.

1908

HENRY FORD'S VISION BECAME REALITY AS THE VERY FIRST MODEL T was shipped from his Piquette Avenue plant on Oct. 1. With top speeds of 45 mph and the backbone to handle the rugged roads of the day, the $300 Lizzie became the "universal car" that sent millions whizzing from the farm to the city. It was offered in nine body styles, all on the same chassis (including the 1915 Town Car, shown here in front of the Michigan Central Depot). Well before the Model T faded into history in May 1927, the Ford nameplate was on half the cars in the world.

1910   WHEN THE SUBJECT TURNS TO DETROIT'S PARKS, BELLE ISLE TENDS TO NAB all the attention. But Palmer Park, on the city's north side, has plenty of its own amenities: tennis courts, a golf course, baseball diamonds and the Merrill Fountain, along with rustic woods containing a winsome log cabin. Another attraction is the lighthouse, surrounded by a duck pond, where these two women are soaking up the atmosphere. In winter, the frozen pond is transformed into a skating rink. Situated just south of McNichols and running north to Seven Mile, the park is named after Sen. Thomas Palmer, who owned the property in the 19th century. In 1893, he and his wife donated 130 acres of their 725-acre estate to the city for park development. Palmer's first speech to the U.S. Senate in 1884 focused on support of women's suffrage — decades before women won the right to vote. In 1920, the city bought additional land from the former Palmer estate, and the park and its environs expanded. Starting in the booming 1920s, tony apartment buildings sprang up around the south side of the park. Just north of the park stands Palmer Woods, probably the city's most elegant neighborhood. On the park's western rim runs Pontchartrain Drive, dotted with stately homes. The area is also notable for the country's first mile of paved concrete, running between McNichols and Seven Mile on Woodward. Of course, the park has changed through the years, but it remains one of the city's greatest charms.

1910 NOT BEING ABLE TO AFFORD AN AUTOMOBILE SHOULDN'T KEEP A PERSON OR four from being photographed in one — or at least a cardboard facsimile. That was the philosophy of downtown entrepreneurs like A.C. Dietsche, who offered sightseeing tours, postcards, souvenirs and practically anything else of interest to the out-of-town visitor, back in the days when Detroit actually was a major tourist destination.

1910

By mid-March, Michigan-weather neophytes may think winter is behind us; after all, that's when spring arrives. But those who've experienced Detroit's seasonal schizophrenia know that the calendar is often misleading. In fact, the biggest Detroit snowfall on record happened on April 6, 1886, when the city was clobbered with more than 2 feet of snow, with drifts climbing much higher than that. The year 1910, when this photo was taken, was not Detroit's snowiest year. That notoriety, according to the *Detroit Free Press' The Detroit Almanac*, belongs to 1880-81, when 93.6 inches pummeled Detroit. (The annual average is about 41 inches.) But 1910 did have an unusual claim to meteorological fame: On May 31, flakes fell, making it the latest city snowfall on record. And on May 9, 1923, a half-foot blanketed the city.

1912

STARTING IN 1916, THE THREE BOOK BROTHERS — ASSISTED BY ARCHITECT Louis Kemper — changed a deteriorating residential street called Washington Avenue into a fashionable boulevard of soaring office buildings, luxury hotels and upscale shops. Josephine Fox Fink, who worked as a stenographer downtown in the 1920s, recalled Washington Boulevard in its heyday: "Sax-Kay Shop, Himelhoch's, Higgins & Frank — *that* was high-toned shopping." The Books erected the Book-Cadillac Hotel and the 36-story Book Tower in the 1920s, but plans for a 70-story skyscraper were shelved by the Great Depression. For years, Washington Boulevard was the site of a popular local landmark — the ice fountain. Several jets were allowed to play all winter, resulting in tons of crystal and a massive berg of ice that at times reached heights of 30 feet and more. The famous ice fountain, along with the two anonymous (but fashionable) ladies standing in front of it some 90 years ago, are long gone. But here, at least, all remain frozen in time.

1912

HALLOWEEN IS NORMALLY A TIME FOR FUN AND FRIVOLITY, BUT THESE YOUNG women had a serious bent. Instead of trick-or-treating as princesses or witches, Hamtramck resident Alvina Wilke (right) and her socially conscious friends dressed up as suffragettes. The girls were about 13 or 14 at the time, when women were dis-enfranchised. Women's suffrage leaders such as Elizabeth Cady Stanton and Susan B. Anthony, who were both dead by 1912, no doubt would have been proud of the budding activists. These Hamtramck girls would not have to wait too long before their demands were heard, however. The 19th Amendment to the Constitution granted American women the right to vote in 1920.

1912 WHEN BUYING A THANKSGIVING TURKEY, MOST OF US OPT FOR THE EASY ROUTE: buying a frozen bird at the supermarket, which requires little more than defrosting, stuffing, seasoning and basting it. But in an earlier era, it wasn't always such a simple task. Shoppers sometimes bought live fowl, which involved plucking, cleaning — and chopping off the hapless bird's head. This woman shopping at Eastern Market for her family's Thanksgiving meal probably would have to perform those unfortunate tasks. Of course, turkey is the conventional main course on Thanksgiving, but for Europeans, goose to this day remains a popular entrée for holiday meals. Detroit was teeming with immigrants in 1912, and this shawled woman carrying a live goose could very well have hailed from the Old World. But whether it's turkey, goose or a meatless meal, Thanksgiving dinner just isn't complete without a generous serving of good company.

1914

STREETCARS MAY NOT HAVE BEEN THE MOST GLAMOROUS MODE OF TRANS-portation, but they served their purpose exceedingly well: They took people where they wanted to go. Ever since the 1890s, when the first Detroit trolley rolled out on Jefferson Avenue, commuters depended on them as a reliable ride. Day and night, white-collar office workers and factory workers alike crammed onto the busy cars, from the crosstown Warren Avenue line to the well-traveled Grand River and Woodward routes. The clang of the trolley bells and the screeching sound of the cars riding the rails contributed to the urban cacophony of a bustling city. This photo of Michigan Avenue shows the confluence of three manners of transportation — past, present and future. The old-fashioned method, a horse-drawn cart (left foreground) is pictured alongside streetcars and the most recent form of transport, the automobile. Although cars and trolleys continue to share the road in cities like San Francisco and Toronto, automobiles eventually replaced streetcars in Detroit. Many believed there was even collusion among the Big Three to derail the trolleys. Whatever the reason, the Detroit street-cars rode their final routes in 1956 and were sold to Mexico City.

1915

THE THOUGHT OF RESTRICTIVE MANACLES, ROPES AND CHAINS INSTILLS FEAR and panic in most people, but Harry Houdini, seen here circa 1915 while performing one of his astounding feats, wasn't most people. The ultimate escape artist, Houdini (born Ehrich Weiss in 1874) reveled in freeing himself from the most confining obstacles. Houdini staged wild publicity stunts, garnering him an iconic status — and screaming headlines — around the world. In Detroit, in November 1906, shackled by Detroit Police Department handcuffs and tied to a lifeline, Houdini jumped from the Belle Isle Bridge into the bone-chilling, dangerous currents of the Detroit River. He escaped and swam to safety. Twenty years later, again in Detroit, Houdini's defiance of death would finally fail him. After a show at the Garrick Theatre (on Griswold, long since demolished), Houdini, complaining of pain and a high fever, was rushed to Grace Hospital, where it was determined he had peritonitis. The previous week, while in his dressing room in Montreal, Houdini had been visited by a young man who asked if it was true that Houdini could sustain repeated punches to his abdomen. Houdini was sorting his mail at the time and wasn't able to prepare himself; the repeated blows ruptured the performer's appendix. Houdini died on Oct. 31 in Room 401 at Grace. For a decade afterward, his wife, Bess, conducted a yearly séance on Halloween, hoping to summon Houdini's spirit. It didn't work. But the great showman, ever mindful of the power of publicity, just may be waiting for the right time.

1916 FRENCH SETTLERS CALLED IT ISLE AU COCHONS (HOG ISLAND), SO NAMED for its porcine population. But given the island's abundant natural beauty, the sobriquet wasn't entirely fitting. In 1845, a more appropriate name was bestowed — Belle Isle, reportedly honoring Michigan Gov. Lewis Cass' daughter, Isabelle. After the city bought the land for $200,000 in 1879, Frederick Law Olmsted (who planned New York's Central Park) was hired to design the grounds. Soon, the island blossomed with natural and man-made amenities, including a casino, a conservatory, a children's zoo, the Detroit Yacht Club, the Scott Fountain and the Dossin Great Lakes Museum. Swimming, picnicking and canoeing lured thousands of harried Detroiters to the verdant oasis. That was the case even in 1916, when this photo captured canoeists enjoying a lazy day. Belle Isle has seen better days, and there's intermittent talk of an entry fee to help maintain the island. But for now, it's one of the few places left where it doesn't cost a penny to unwind on a languorous afternoon.

1918 THE FACES ON THESE YOUNG MEN FROM HAMTRAMCK HIGH SCHOOL ARE somber, even a little threatening — but maybe they just took football seriously. Or perhaps their school spirit for the Hamtramck Cosmos was simply intense. Of course, today's jerseys and helmets look nothing like the uniforms of all those decades ago, but the game continues unchanged as an autumn ritual. Hamtramck, a suburb within Detroit's boundaries, has always been a town of immigrants, chiefly Polish. To this day, there's still a strong Polish contingent, but there's also a potent mix of other cultures, including arrivals from Albania and Yemen. The Hamtramck High School on Hewett Street these players represented, built in 1914, has been gone for several years, says Edward Malczewski, principal of Hamtramck High, adding that the current high school on Charest once was Copernicus Junior High School.

1921   BEFORE THERE WAS EASTWOOD PARK ON THE EAST SIDE AND EDGEWATER PARK on the west side, Detroit's thrill-seekers got their kicks at Electric Park, located just west of the Belle Isle Bridge (later named the MacArthur Bridge). Opened in 1906 and built by insurance mogul Arthur Gaukler, the seven-acre park, lit by 75,000 electric bulbs, gave New York's Coney Island a run for its money. Merrymakers toured the House of Nemo, a topsy-turvy fun house; zipped along on a roller coaster with 14 peaks; and cruised down an 85-foot-high maple spiral slide called the Down and Out Tower. There also were hot-air balloon races, parachute drops and a 5,000-seat theater featuring opera and drama. A huge pier over the Detroit River was a popular meeting place before it burned down in 1921. After Gaukler died in 1912, Henry Ford bought the property from his widow. It changed hands — and names — several times, going by Pike's Peak, Riverside and Granada Park. By 1928, the plug finally was pulled on Electric Park, and demolition was completed the next year. The thrill, as B.B. King would say, was gone.

1922

TODAY, THE AUTO INDUSTRY IS DOMINATED BY JUST A FEW PLAYERS. BUT IN the early 20th century there were scads of car companies, many of them located in Detroit. One was the Chalmers Motor Car Co., begun in 1908 by Hugh Chalmers, a former vice president with the National Cash Register Co. In its early years, the firm was known as Chalmers-Detroit, but by 1910 the "Detroit" was dropped. The Chalmers developed a reputation as a racing car, but it was also popular with the public, demonstrated by this stylish woman stepping into a 1923 model Chalmers. According to a Michigan Inspection Bureau report from 1913, the Chalmers factory on East Jefferson employed 2,500 during the day and 150 workers at night. The best year, though, was 1916, when 21,000 of the autos left the factory. The company nabbed a good deal of publicity when it awarded the most valuable player in baseball with a new Chalmers. Detroit Tiger Ty Cobb was the first to win the Chalmers Award in 1911. The firm wasn't destined for a long life, however. The recession after World War I hit Chalmers hard, and it merged with the equally troubled Maxwell Motor Corp. The union lasted about as long as a Hollywood marriage, though, and Walter P. Chrysler absorbed the company in 1924.

1925 THROW A PARTY IN DETROIT DURING PROHIBITION AND YOU NEVER KNOW who'll show up. One evening, contractor and sportsman Alfred Tenge (number 7 in photo) gathered friends and guests in the basement of his house on Hubbell Street for some homemade brew and lively conversation. Familiar faces include Blanche Martin (first woman from the left), a *Harper's Bazaar* model and editor; her married lover, Detroit Tigers outfielder Harry Heilmann (number 9), who is doing his best to hide his face from the camera; and none other than Babe Ruth, whose long-distance home runs made him the most famous man in America.

1926

TODAY, MOUNT CLEMENS MAY NOT SEEM LIKE MUCH OF A TOURIST DESTI-nation. But for decades, beginning around 1870, thousands flocked here, includ-ing Babe Ruth, Mae West, Jack Dempsey, William Randolph Hearst and Henry Ford. They all came for the curative powers of Mount Clemens' heated mineral baths, pumped from some 1,400 feet under the city. The restorative waters were said to relieve arthritis, eczema, polio, even syphilis. A robust massage would typically follow a soaking. Soon, the town earned the nickname "Bath City," and a slew of elegant hotels, including the Hotel Murphy Baths (shown here in a circa mid-'20s photo) sprang up to accommodate pilgrims. However helpful the baths may have been, they certainly didn't smell like a gardenia patch. The sulfurous waters emitted a stench like rotten eggs. The Great Depression took its toll, and the introduction of penicillin in the '40s and the Salk polio vaccine in the early '50s turned the bath industry into a trickle. The last bath house, the Arethusa, closed in 1974. The grand old hotels have been razed. But Debbie Larsen, assistant director of the Mount Clemens Public Library, says there's still a vestige of the bath era — St. Joseph Hospital on North Avenue, formerly St. Joseph Sanitarium, which once included a bath house. Larsen says the baths were resumed as a form of physical therapy.

1926

IN THE 1920s, LIBRARIES OFTEN WERE OPULENTLY DESIGNED STRUCTURES with high ceilings, ornate plasterwork and marble pillars, their walls festooned with murals containing quotes from civilization's great thinkers. The mere scale of the buildings projected an ambience suited for the attainment of knowledge. Their majestic facades exuded a propensity for classical style and erudition; just think of the stately Main Detroit Public Library or Highland Park's McGregor Public Library, places possessing a Parnassus-like appeal. But one can read and learn with equal fervor in more humble structures, of course. The Down-river city of Ecorse, once a resort community, was experiencing a boom in the steel industry in the '20s, but this unassuming library seems a throwback to simpler, more rustic times. Modest or august, all libraries serve the same purpose: to broaden the imagination, fortify the mind and foster dreams — ideals one suspects were embraced by the young people pictured here more than three-quarters of a century ago in front of the Ecorse Public Library.

1929 Rising majestically across the Detroit River (152 feet high at its center and 9,200 feet long from entrance to exit), the Ambassador Bridge is an enduring landmark — not just of Detroit, but of two nations. Linking Canada and the United States, the bridge serves as an international gateway between two powerful trading partners. In fact, more than a quarter of the merchandise moving between the countries crosses the bridge. But scores of other travelers on pleasure trips traverse the bridge, too. In this shot, crowds jam the Ambassador on its opening day: Nov. 11, 1929. Even though the stock market crashed two weeks earlier, plucky Detroiters turned out by the tens of thousands for the dedication ceremony. At the time, it was the longest suspension bridge in the world. The Ambassador Bridge has been the scene of many dramas, from suicides to weddings to publicity stunts. Although there have been many cosmetic changes to the bridge through the years, the most striking was the 1981 addition of a necklace of lights lacing around the cables, adding a decidedly romantic touch to the evening skyline.

1930   IT USED TO BE THAT EVERY HOUSE CONTAINED A MILK CHUTE FOR DELIVERIES of cold milk in glass bottles, fresh cream in half-pint bottles, eggs, cottage cheese and other dairy products. Until the 1960s, it was common to spot creamery trucks every morning making their rounds, with milkmen in crisp white uniforms toting metal crates up walkways or driveways. Creameries, both locally and nationally owned, once were scattered all over the city, and so were their trucks. Brown's, Twin Pines, Brickley's, Eagle, United, Foremost, Sealtest and Borden's were some of the more memorable names. Back in the '30s, Belle Isle Creamery Co., located on East Forest, was among a slew of Detroit dairies. This photo shows a Belle Isle milkman on duty, serving residents of these spacious homes on West Grand Boulevard near Linwood. What was an everyday sight is now a rarity; there are far fewer creameries today, and only a handful make home deliveries.

1930

SUMMER IS A TIME FOR LAZY PICNICS IN THE SUN, AND FEW COULD BE more lavish than this elegant spread at a surprise party for Hiram Walker Jr. on the grounds of his posh Grosse Pointe Farms home. In those days, guests dressed up for parties — even if they were held outdoors. A more informal atmosphere can be seen around the pool at the rear, where swimwear consisted of tank tops for men and bathing caps for women. Walker belonged to the famous whiskey-producing Hiram Walker Distillers family, whose headquarters still stand on the Windsor riverfront. Walker lived on Provencal Road, among the most desirable addresses in the Pointes. Provencal retains its exclusivity today. The private road, adorned with stately mansions and wending around the golf course of the Country Club of Detroit, is home to some of the most notable families in the region.

1934

ASK ANYONE TO NAME AMERICAN AUTO MANUFACTURERS AND THE BIG Three leap to mind. But until the middle of the 20th century, there were several competitors. Factories that made Packard, Hupp, Hudson and other cars dotted Detroit's industrial landscape. The Hudson Motor Car Co., in business from 1909-1954, was founded by a group that included Howard Coffin, Roy Chapin and Joseph L. Hudson — the latter of the J.L. Hudson department store fame and the automaker's chief bankroller. The Hudson cars proved popular with the public, and the Terraplane was its most famous model. In this photo, Hudson autoworkers put the finishing touches on the 1934 Terraplane Challenger series at the Hudson plant at Conner and Jefferson on the city's east side. Hudson merged with Nash-Kelvinator in 1954, creating a new auto company, American Motors. The old Hudson plant was demolished in 1961.

1935

OF ALL THE BUILDINGS THAT HAVE BEEN RAZED IN DETROIT, ONE OF THE most lamented is Old City Hall, which stood on what is now Kennedy Square. The 19th and 20th centuries collide in this photo, as the Guardian and Penobscot buildings hover commandingly over City Hall. The stately building, erected in 1871, included sandstone sculptures of the civic virtues — justice, industry, art and commerce — at the base of its cupola, as well as sculptures of Cadillac and other early settlers. They were carved by Detroit artist Julius Melchers, the father of artist Gari Melchers, who would gain worldwide fame for his portraits and landscapes. In 1955, City Hall was abandoned for the spanking-new City-County Building in the burgeoning Civic Center. In September of that year, Mayor Albert Cobo and a cadre of city officials marched down Woodward to the new digs. Old City Hall, as it became affectionately known, met the wrecker's ball in 1961, the same year that 31-year-old Jerome Cavanagh became mayor of Detroit.

1935

MANY FIRST LADIES ARE CONTENT TO HOST TEA PARTIES AND ATTEND TO other ceremonial duties at the White House. Not Eleanor Roosevelt. A social crusader, writer and world traveler, the wife of President Franklin Delano Roosevelt capitalized on her role to promote humanitarian causes. In 1939, Mrs. Roosevelt arranged for the black contralto Marian Anderson to sing at the Lincoln Memorial after the Daughters of the American Revolution banned Anderson from performing at Constitution Hall — which the DAR owned — because of her race. In this shot, Mrs. Roosevelt is seen attending the clearance of slums on Benton Street in Detroit while a young admirer makes her acquaintance. Even after the death of her husband in 1945, Mrs. Roosevelt continued to be active in public service. President Truman, who dubbed her "first lady of the world," appointed her a member of the U.S. delegation to the United Nations. Among her contributions was helping to found UNICEF. Aside from her syndicated daily newspaper column, "My Day," Mrs. Roosevelt wrote several books. She remained an influential force in the Democratic Party until she died in 1962.

1936 WHEN HE WASN'T BUSY DISPENSING PILLS AT HIS DOWNTOWN DETROIT pharmacy, James Vernor liked to experiment at his drugstore's soda fountain. In the early 1860s, he concocted a refreshing drink of 19 ingredients, the most salient flavors being ginger and vanilla. When he was called to serve in the Civil War, Vernor kept the concoction aging in an oak barrel. Upon his return, a new soft drink was born — Vernor's Ginger Ale — which was sold beginning in 1866. For years, thirsty Detroiters visited the Vernor's bottling plant on the riverfront, near the Bob-Lo dock. In this photo, a crowd assembles to toast Vernor's on its 70th anniversary. The plant moved to Woodward Avenue in 1954, just north of the Cultural Center, where the trademark Vernor's gnome and oak barrel graced a huge sign. In 1966, the company was sold, and is now part of the Texas-based Dr Pepper/Seven Up Inc. Although the tangible ties to Detroit have been severed, Vernor's, with its nose-tingling carbonation and gingery kick, will be associated forever with the city.

1936 IT SEEMS THAT THE MOST POPULAR WINTER SPORT IS COMPLAINING ABOUT the snow and cold. But carping only seems to tighten winter's grip. Hardy souls know that the easiest way to endure the season is to join forces with it, as these skaters on Belle Isle did in the mid-'30s. There are few more bracing ways to spend a chilly winter afternoon than to pass the time ice-skating as large flakes fall lazily from the sky. For decades, Belle Isle has been a welcome spot for skaters eager to glide along the ice leisurely or boldly attempt a double axel. On an outdoor rink, there's an egalitarian spirit; tyros have the same claim to the ice as experts. Accomplished speed skaters might whoosh by like a locomotive, leaving a comet of ice shavings behind them, while a wobbly-legged neophyte, resembling a newborn pony, valiantly tries to negotiate his way. Sure, there are indoor rinks, and the quality of ice there is invariably better, but skating outdoors somehow is just more fun.

1936 EASTERN MARKET HAS BEEN AROUND FOR MORE THAN 160 YEARS (113 IN its current location on Russell near Gratiot), but its Old World flavor remains intact. Well before dawn, farmers and vendors bring their fruits and vegetables, live animals, herbs and such to sell. In addition, shopkeepers in 19th-century buildings peddle wine, spices, cheeses, nuts, meats and candy. Most people visit the market on Saturdays, but farmers do their main business during the week, when merchants buy their supplies at wholesale. In the above photo, shoppers and farmers do business amid bushels of produce. Eastern Market, open year-round, also is famed for its colorful Flower Day in May, as well as Oktoberfest. And at Christmastime, the pungent scent of pine pervades the air, as customers haggle over trees, wreaths and garlands. Before 1891, the market was in Cadillac Square, but it moved to the current site when downtown became too congested. The history of the Eastern Market area itself is teeming with interest. The Russell Street Cemetery once stood on the land, and bodies were exhumed and moved to other grounds before the market moved in. In the 1860s, the Detroit House of Correction and the House of Shelter for Women were built on the site. Belle Starr, the notorious outlaw, spent time in the slammer there. There's a military connection, too: Generals Ulysses S. Grant and George Custer once marched their troops in the area.

1937

NO ONE COULD HAVE GUESSED IN 1896 THAT WHEN HE BROUGHT HIS RICK-ety "quadricycle" out for a spin from his Bagley Avenue garage, Henry Ford would soon put the world on wheels. Even Ford was surprised that the flivver moved. "The darn thing ran!" he said incredulously. In 1903, Ford Motor Co. was incorporated, beginning its operations on Mack Avenue. The fledgling but growing company then relocated to Piquette and Beaubien, only to move again to Highland Park, where Albert Kahn built the world's largest automobile plant in 1909. A year before, Ford started production of the wildly popular Model T. In this shot, taken on Jan. 18, 1937, to celebrate Ford's 25 millionth automobile, Henry Ford sits in the original buggy he built while son Edsel perches behind the wheel of a new Ford. The company has continued on the fast track. In November of 2003, Ford Chairman and CEO Bill Ford Jr. drove the company's 300 millionth vehicle — a 2004 red Mustang GT ragtop — off the assembly line.

1938

NEARLY 40 YEARS BEFORE THE RENAISSANCE CENTER FIRST DOMINATED THE Detroit skyline, 22 years before Cobo Hall began to serve conventioneers and 17 years before the opening of Ford Auditorium, the view from Windsor already was that of an imposing urban center. Vernor's still operated its plant on the riverfront, and passengers alighting from the Bob-Lo boats commonly stopped in for a ginger-ale float. The central point on the downtown riverfront was almost exactly where Antoine de la Mothe Cadillac founded his settlement on the strait (*le Détroit*) 237 years before.

1939 LONG BEFORE THERE WERE MALLS LIKE SOMERSET, OAKLAND AND LAKESIDE, there was only one place for serious shoppers to go — downtown Detroit. Throngs of people regularly crowded its streets, but at Christmastime the hordes grew exponentially, as this photo of holiday shoppers crossing Woodward attests. Not only did downtown boast the world's tallest department store — Hudson's — but there was also Crowley's and Kern's, as well as budget stores such as Kresge's, Sam's and Woolworth's. All of those emporiums are closed now, and the big department stores have all been leveled, a melancholy fact that in 1939 would seem as improbable as going to the moon.

1939

To look at the abandoned Statler Hotel today, you'd never think that it was once regarded as one of Detroit's most elegant hotels. Its awnings — installed by the city to hide the broken windows when the People Mover passed by — are torn and tattered. But time was when the 1914 structure on Washington Boulevard at Grand Circus Park was indeed a place where the elite would meet. Not only was it a draw for out-of-towners, but native Detroiters also partook of the Statler's amenities. Every posh hotel had a grand restaurant, and the Statler's Terrace Room attracted everyone from businessmen and downtown shoppers to the socially conscious ladies who lunch — refined matrons who knew, in 1939, that it was *de rigueur* to don a hat when dining out, as this picture of a long-vanished era reveals.

1942

IT WASN'T AS LARGE OR EXTENSIVE AS HUDSON'S, BUT CROWLEY'S DEPARTMENT store in downtown Detroit was nevertheless a classy emporium that catered to varied tastes. Built in 1907 at Gratiot and Farmer, Crowley's (or Crowley, Milner and Co., as it was known officially) was a must-stop for downtown shoppers. It had the world's first escalators, and the rickety but serviceable wooden convenience remained a quaint fixture through the years. Eventually business dwindled, and the grand white building was razed in 1977. Shoppers took heart in the fact that they could patronize other Crowley's in the area, but even that no longer is an option. In 1999, Crowley's went out of business, joining the roster of other vanished Detroit institutions.

1942 THE TELENEWS THEATRE DISTINGUISHED ITSELF FROM OTHER DOWNTOWN Detroit movie houses in two notable respects. Unlike the palatial theaters constructed in the 1920s, the smaller Telenews was built in 1942 on Woodward, just south of Grand Circus Park. But more remarkable was that the Art Deco-style theater showed only newsreels that, during World War II, were gobbled up by a citizenry hungry for war news in general and reports on the whereabouts of their loved ones in particular. In fact, many moviegoers spotted brothers, husbands or sons overseas in newsreels. In this circa 1942 shot, one gets a sense of the bustle of downtown during the war years. In those pre-TV days, matinees were big business, and the Telenews, like other larger theaters, screened films in the mornings and afternoons. As the marquee attests, the Telenews also housed a basement studio for WXYZ radio. In later years the theater would be renamed the Plaza, which showed mainstream Hollywood films. It also had a brief run as an art-film house. After being closed for several years, the theater re-emerged as a nightclub.

1942

FOR MOST AMERICANS, THANKSGIVING IS A TIME OF BOUNTY, BLESSINGS AND an impressive spread for dinner. But for some, the specter of hunger doesn't take a holiday. However, the good work of the Capuchin Soup Kitchen, on Detroit's east side, has been feeding multitudes of needy people since 1929. More than 60,000 meals are served there every month. In this photo at St. Bonaventure Monastery on Mount Elliott, Father Solanus Casey is at far right preparing a food tray. The mild-mannered Franciscan with a flowing beard was a lowly doorkeeper at the monastery, but many who knew him maintained he held mystical healing powers. Cancer-ridden visitors called upon him and were cured. Others suffering from tuberculosis, diphtheria and other maladies visited him and were well again. Following his death in Detroit in 1957, the Father Solanus Guild gathered evidence of his inexplicable powers. The slow movement toward canonization gained momentum. Should he become a saint, Father Solanus would be the first American-born male to receive the honor. At the very least, the kind friar possessed a charitable and humble nature. It's perhaps no surprise that Father Solanus was born on Thanksgiving Day, 1870, in a log cabin in Wisconsin.

1943

AMERICA — AND MOST OF THE WORLD — WAS ENTRENCHED IN THE MIDDLE of a horrid war, but these six servicemen and women, strolling arm in arm down Lafayette in downtown Detroit, nevertheless found a reason to smile as they made their way to church. After all, it was Easter morning, a time suggestive of hope and rebirth during a very dark time. Known as the Arsenal of Democracy during World War II, Detroit was a busy place in the early '40s, with factories cranking out tanks, planes and munitions day and night until peace arrived in 1945. Still, Detroiters found time to divert their attention from bombs and crazed political leaders. In the background stands the Cass Theatre at Cass and Lafayette (now a parking lot), which showcased the city's top musicals and plays, no doubt brightening the lives of audiences more accustomed to the real-life drama of worldwide conflict.

1944

SEPTEMBER HOLDS VARIOUS ASSOCIATIONS FOR DIFFERENT PEOPLE, BUT TO students it means only one inevitably grim fact: It's back-to-school time. In this picture, male students work on a project in shop class at Detroit's Pershing High School. At that time, when gender roles were more narrowly defined, shop was usually reserved for boys, while girls attended home-economics class. Pershing, at Ryan and Seven Mile, on the city's east side, has one of the most populous student bodies among Detroit's high schools. It was named after Gen. John J. Pershing (1860-1948), who is best known as commander in chief of the American Expeditionary Force in Europe during World War I. American soldiers of The Great War were popularly known as "doughboys," which is also Pershing High's sports team name. Fittingly, Pershing was a schoolteacher in his native Missouri before beginning his military career.

1945 THE CHRISTMAS SEASON NO DOUBT ACCOUNTED FOR THE HAPPY DEMEANOR of these downtown Detroit shoppers, and perhaps some even were mugging for the camera. But they were genuinely elated that World War II was behind them, accompanied by a heady patriotism that boosted the spirits of U.S. citizens. The enormous expense of the war still had to be financed, however, which explains the war bond posters hanging from the street lamps. Taken at Woodward and State on Dec. 1, 1945, this photo shows how packed downtown once was, especially at Christmas. Looking north on Woodward, the sea of people seems endless. The retail was vast, including such stores as Hudson's, Crowley's, Kern's, Himelhoch's, Grinnell's, B. Siegel, Wright Kay and scores of others. Back in the '40s, if you couldn't find a particular gift downtown, it probably didn't exist.

1946 AFTER LEARNING TO MAKE SACRIFICES BECAUSE OF FOOD RATIONING during World War II, these shoppers look eager to place their orders at the butcher counter. Sugar, butter, meat and other foodstuffs were once limited, but a year after the war's end supplies were again plentiful, and Americans were free to buy what they pleased. This photo was taken on May 23, 1946, during a busy moment at the Wrigley's supermarket on Plymouth near Asbury Park, on Detroit's northwest side. Wrigley's was among a chain of markets once operating in metro Detroit. But like Packer, Food Fair, C.F. Smith, Chatham and other grocers, Wrigley's rang up its last sale years ago.

~~~~~~~~

1948 WHEN JOE DIMAGGIO DIED AT 84 OF LUNG CANCER IN MARCH 1999, clichés ran rampant. There were numerous references to his nicknames — Joltin' Joe and The Yankee Clipper — and countless snippets of Simon and Garfunkel's mawkish 1967 song "Mrs. Robinson," a few lines of which paid tribute to DiMaggio. Trite words like "legendary" and "hero" were splashed across newspaper tributes. All of which is ironic, because DiMaggio was the farthest thing from a cliché — no one could imitate his overall expertise on the field. There was that astonishing 56-game hitting streak in 1941, the lifetime .325 batting average, the three American League MVP awards, the 10 World Series he played in, and the stats go on. In his 13 years as a New York Yankee, DiMaggio took his game seriously, and it shows in his pensive gaze in this shot taken during batting practice at Briggs Stadium, later to become Tiger Stadium. Perhaps he was wondering about retiring, which he did three years later. More likely, he was just thinking about playing his best, which he did, admirably and consistently.

1948

THIS STREAMLINED PACKARD BEAUTY, THE SUPER EIGHT CLUB SEDAN, with its "free-flow" styling, powerful eight-cylinder engine and luxurious appointments, helped make 1948 the best sales year Packard had since 1929. The aerodynamic auto, sporting its trademark Goddess of Speed hood ornament, looked as if it were moving even when it was standing still. No wonder the company touted it as "the motor car that makes distance disappear." The Packard Motor Car Co. began in 1899, in Warren, Ohio. But when well-heeled Detroiters Henry Bourne Joy and Truman Newberry invested in the business in 1903, Packard moved up to Detroit. Albert Kahn was hired to design the Packard plant on East Grand Boulevard, a shining example of advanced industrial architecture with reinforced concrete, copious windows and fire-resistant materials. The Packard carried a reputation as a well-built, dependable car, leading to the company's famous slogan: "Ask the man who owns one." The years following 1948 weren't so palmy for Packard. Studebaker took over the ailing company in 1954, and the Detroit plant shuttered in 1956. Studebaker continued to manufacture Packards until 1958.

1949

UNDER ITS 60-FOOT VAULTED CEILINGS IS A STOREHOUSE OF MEMORIES. IT was the scene of tearful goodbyes and jubilant welcomes, of harried departures and happy-to-be-home arrivals. Businessmen, servicemen and travelers of every stripe bustled across its Welsh quarry-tile floors and under its Romanesque arches, going to or coming from New York, Baltimore, Chicago or dozens of other cities. Since its opening in 1913 and continuing through many decades, Detroit's Michigan Central Depot was a scene of perpetual hurly-burly. But even before its doors closed in 1988, train travel had fallen out of favor, considered too slow for a world intent on getting nowhere fast. Gone, too, was the romance of rail travel, of looking dreamily out the window and drinking up the scenery. From a distance, the old station on Vernor at Michigan rises majestically, but the once-elegant building has been badly vandalized. Talk of turning the structure into a casino or a hotel fizzled out. It seemed headed for demolition, its fate as sad as the lonesome wail of a train's siren in the night. Then came an 11th-hour reprieve. In 2004, Mayor Kwame Kilpatrick announced plans to transform Michigan Central Depot into Detroit Police Headquarters.

1950

TO THE DISAPPOINTMENT OF MANY CHILDREN, SEPTEMBER IS BACK-TO-school month. Even for grown-ups, the smell of freshly sharpened pencils and the sound of chalk gliding across a blackboard will be forever linked with early school days. This 1950 kindergarten class at Grosse Pointe Shores' Vernier School was typical of classrooms a half-century ago; there's not a computer terminal in sight. The Vernier School, at Vernier and Lake Shore roads, was designed by Albert Kahn and opened in 1916. The school closed in 1956 and was used for storage and as a polling precinct by the Village of Grosse Pointe Shores. It also had a 10-year run as a co-op nursery school, from 1958-68. But the aging building's days were numbered, and it was demolished in 1994. There are remaining vestiges of the Vernier School, however. The school's bell was salvaged and is on display with an accompanying plaque on the building's former site. Also, bricks from the school adorn the welcome signs in Grosse Pointe Shores.

VERNIER
GRADE SCHOOL
KINDERGARTEN
MAY 3 1950
GROSS POINTE
2

1950

DETROIT'S SCARAB CLUB, AT 217 FARNSWORTH, JUST EAST OF THE DETROIT Institute of Arts, has long been a haven for artists and arts patrons. Although the Northern Italian Renaissance building was erected in 1928, the organization has existed since 1907, when it was known as the Hopkin Club, in honor of Detroit artist Robert Hopkin. The club began as a gathering place for artists, musicians and architects, but included artists' studios on the top floor as well as sketching classes in the basement — just as it does today. Visitors to monthly exhibits are often drawn to the second-floor lounge, where the signatures of such notable artists as John Sloan, Diego Rivera, Marcel Duchamp and Norman Rockwell are scrawled into the crossbeams. The organization's name was changed to the Scarab Club in 1910. The scarab, an Egyptian symbol of rebirth, can be seen in a beautiful Pewabic logo on the building's facade. One of the traditions at the club was the Beaux Arts Ball, which began in 1917 at the old Addison Hotel. "There was always a theme, and the artists got together and painted murals and made decorations to fit that theme," says Patricia Reed, Scarab Club president and archivist. In 1950, when this photo of festive dancers was taken, the theme was "The Parade of Nations." Reed says the balls were an annual event from 1920 through 1950, then became sporadic affairs. In 2000, the ball returned and was so successful that it again became an annual event.

1951

DETROITERS LOVE AN EXCUSE TO THROW A PARTY. WORLD SERIES VICTORIES, Stanley Cup wins, Thanksgiving and Labor Day parades, as well as Cinco de Mayo and St. Patrick's Day celebrations have brought out hordes of jubilant people throughout the years. Sometimes, though, the reason for a toast has a historical dimension. Here, the occasion was the 250th birthday of the founding of Detroit by Antoine de la Mothe Cadillac and his retinue in July of 1701. In July 1951, downtown Detroit was packed with enthusiasts who came to watch a parade depicting the history of the city. Fittingly, the new Detroit Historical Museum also opened in the same month at Woodward and Kirby.

1951

In this age of chronic complaint, it's humbling to remember, at Thanksgiving, the disadvantaged or impoverished — many of whom nevertheless find reason to give thanks. This photo from the Sarah Fisher Home for Orphans shows children (and one sweet baby) saying grace before their Thanksgiving dinner spread. Some are even dressed like pilgrims. Today, the St. Vincent and Sarah Fisher Center in Farmington Hills carries on its good work, caring for abused and neglected children ages 4-17 and striving to find permanent homes for them. The nonprofit organization also provides post-adoption support services and outreach for unwed mothers and young fathers. The Center traces its beginnings to the 19th century, when the Daughters of Charity arrived in Detroit and opened St. Vincent's Academy.

1953

BEFORE THE JOINT OPERATING AGREEMENT BETWEEN "THE DETROIT NEWS" and the *Detroit Free Press* went into effect in 1989, the two papers were engaged in a fierce news and circulation battle. But there was a time when a third opponent made the circulation war even more intense. *The Detroit Times*, published between 1900 and 1960, trailed behind *The News* and *Freep* in readership, but *The Times* had some top-notch reporters, including Ray Girardin (who went on to become Detroit's police commissioner) and Don Ball (who later went to *The News*), who kept the competing papers' journalists on their toes — sometimes even scooping them. *The Times*, a Hearst newspaper since 1921, had a special affinity for crime and corruption coverage, and its screaming headlines delighted readers. The afternoon paper's offices were in downtown Detroit on Times Square. It waged a valiant fight, but the publication finally folded in November of 1960 when the rival *Detroit News* bought it. *The News* continued to use *The Times*' printing presses for years, but the stately building was razed in the 1970s.

1954

LONG BEFORE THE WORD DIVERSITY BECAME COMMON, IT WAS THE GUIDING principle of the International Institute of Metropolitan Detroit. The organization was founded in 1919, and its purpose, says Executive Director Dick Thibodeau, "is to aid immigrants and foster understanding between cultures." Each year, the International Institute sponsored a Folk Ball, which Thibodeau says "celebrated the rich ethnic traditions in metro Detroit." In this photograph, shot in the ballroom of Detroit's Masonic Temple, former Gov. G. Mennen "Soapy" Williams (first row, center) leads the "Grand March" with his wife, Nancy, as others — many dressed in ethnic garb — follow. Eventually, the Folk Balls were absorbed into today's Annual World Market, held during the Detroit Festival of the Arts. Williams, who served as Michigan's Democratic governor from 1949-1960, continued his interest in international matters. He served as U.S. Ambassador to the Philippines and as U.S. Undersecretary of State for African Affairs in the 1960s. Williams got the name "Soapy" because of his association with the Mennen family, which produces shaving cream and other toiletries. Williams, who served on the Michigan Supreme Court from 1970-1987, died in 1988. That same year, the International Institute inducted him into its International Heritage Hall of Fame, a permanent exhibit at Cobo Hall.

1954

ORIGINALLY BUILT AS AN AUTOMOTIVE SHOWPLACE AT THE 1933-34 Chicago World's Fair, the Ford Rotunda was dismantled and moved to Schaefer Road in Dearborn, where it served as an exhibition hall. In the '50s, it was the fifth most popular tourist destination in the United States. Beginning in 1953, the site was transformed each holiday season into an enchanting Christmas Fantasy, drawing millions of visitors. The festive displays changed each year, from an assembly line of animated elves making toys one year to a 15,000-piece miniature circus in another. But the chief attraction was always a huge Nativity scene with life-size figures of the Holy Family, the Magi and shepherds in a desert setting. Of course, Santa Claus also was on hand, and the towering, 40-foot Christmas tree was a constant, too. Little girls were awestruck by the array of thousands of dolls — dressed by Ford women — that were distributed by the Goodfellows to underprivileged children just before Christmas. The Fantasy came to a sad conclusion when the Rotunda went up in flames in November of 1962, leaving the building in ruins in less than an hour.

1954

MANY PEOPLE REMEMBER THE DOWNTOWN HUDSON'S AND CROWLEY'S, but fewer recall Kern's department store, seen here at night decorated for Christmas. Kern's trademark was its clock, and downtown shoppers were fond of saying, "I'll meet you under the Kern's clock." In 1893, Ernst Kern founded his store on St. Antoine. A year later, it moved to Randolph Street. Finally, in 1897, the store relocated to Woodward and Gratiot. Business was brisk at Kern's, so a larger edifice was built on the same site in 1919 — right next to its major competitor, Hudson's. Sadly, Kern's went out of business in 1959. During the urban renewal trend, Kern's was razed — along with the neighboring block at Campus Martius and Woodward — in 1966. Another slice of history is captured in this photo: streetcar tracks and wires, which would disappear in a couple of years. Although Kern's is just a memory, the famous clock was salvaged, and it still stands on Woodward today.

1954

DETROITERS FLOCKED TO DOWNTOWN HUDSON'S FOR VARIOUS REASONS. Readers gravitated to the store's extensive book department. Audiophiles headed to the record department, where shoppers could listen to the latest releases on headphones — long before that service became commonplace. Fashionable women admired the latest styles in the posh Woodward Shops. Hungry diners made a bee-line for the Riverview Room to savor a signature Maurice salad or chicken pot pie. For kids, though, there was only one place to go: Toyland, on Hudson's 12th floor. The area was entrancing year-round, but at Christmas it became absolutely magical. In scope and variety, it resembled Santa's own haven at the North Pole, complete with lavish holiday decorations. In this photo, Santa and his team of reindeer are suspended from the ceiling, keeping vigil over Hudson's vast array of toys. Toyland will be lodged forever in the memory of its visitors, but it remains only that — a memory. The downtown emporium — the world's tallest department store — closed in 1983 and was imploded in October of 1998. Even the name Hudson's is erased; Marshall Field's replaced the signage at all Hudson's stores in 2001.

1955

TIME WAS WHEN DETROITERS REALLY KNEW HOW TO HAVE FUN. AMUSEment parks, including Walled Lake Amusement Park and Casino, Jefferson Beach, Bob-Lo, Eastwood Park and Edgewater Park, dotted the metro area. Edgewater, so named because it sat at the edge of the Rouge River, opened in 1927 on Seven Mile just east of Telegraph in Detroit. Like other amusement parks, Edgewater devoted some of its rides to kiddies, such as this scaled-down roller coaster. The wailing tyke in the second car, however, doesn't appear to be having such a great time. The park also had an adult-version roller coaster, called the Wild Beast, which in later years became the Soul Train. The Giant Octopus and the Wild Mouse were other big draws. Edgewater was also a hot date site, and teenagers flocked to the place on Friday and Saturday nights. In 1961, a little-known singer named Barbra Streisand, who was in town for a gig at downtown's Caucus Club, recorded a radio commercial for Edgewater Park. The thrills lasted until the early 1980s, when the last dodge 'em car crashed at Edgewater.

1956

MOST DETROIT SUBURBS SPRANG UP IN THE YEARS FOLLOWING WORLD WAR II, but Ferndale, just north of Detroit, was incorporated as a village in 1918 and as a city in 1927. Many of its houses were built in the 1920s and '30s. By mid-century, Ferndale and other more established suburbs such as Royal Oak, Wyandotte, Birmingham, Highland Park and Grosse Pointe had their own modest but bustling downtowns. Although there were several Ferndale businesses on Woodward, such as Federal's Department Store (now Old Navy) and the Radio City Theatre (now demolished), West Nine Mile Road was — and remains — a thriving artery as well. Then as now, several restaurants and stores operate on the strip. But the businesses in this photo from almost a half-century ago — Ferndale Lanes, Mode O'Day, S.S. Kresge and Tip Top Good Food — are long gone.

1957 THERE HAS ALWAYS BEEN SOMETHING BITTERSWEET ABOUT THE MICHIGAN State Fair. On the one hand, a trip to the fair is marked by all manner of fun. Live entertainment, carnival rides, prize-winning sheep and horses, witnessing the births of farm animals, prizes for the best blueberry pie, contests for the longest ponytail, and even hog-calling and husband-hollering competitions have been the fair's hallmarks for decades. That's not to mention indulging guiltlessly in calorie overdrive by scarfing down corn dogs, elephant ears, cotton candy and fresh lemonade. Games at makeshift kiosks are also a fair staple, just as they were in 1957, when this photo was shot. But the state fair also sadly signals the end of summer. Perhaps that's why the fairgoers brim with such boundless exuberance, as they try to cram as much activity as they can into the waning summer days. The Michigan State Fair is the nation's oldest, first held in 1849. There have been various fair sites through the years, including Jackson, Kalamazoo, Pontiac and Lansing. But the Michigan State Fair has been held at its current Detroit site, at Eight Mile and Woodward, since 1905, as long as anyone can remember. And tradition is really what the fair is all about.

1960 Eating in one's car is considered a bit gauche today, and some communities even ban the practice. But in the 1950s and '60s, drive-in restaurants were all the rage, particularly among teenagers, who could show off their souped-up wheels while grabbing some cheap grub. Drive-ins were convenient — carhops offered prompt curb service — and diners didn't have to worry about slips in their table manners. On summer nights, rock 'n' roll hits drifted from open car windows or ragtops, adding to the casual ambience. In metro Detroit, one of the most popular drive-ins was the Totem Pole, on Woodward near 10 Mile, in Royal Oak. Woodward Avenue cruisers stopped in to nosh on any number of selections from the Totem Pole's Native American-themed menu: Cherokee Frog Legs, Oneida Fried Clams, Navajo Fresh Ocean Fish, Tepee-style Strawberry Shortcake. Like other drive-ins, the Totem Pole fell victim to changing tastes — and a changing America. Fast-food chains took hold, and the Totem Pole closed in the early 1970s, replaced by a Burger King. However, those with a hankering for a Big Chief Burger, Pocahontas Roast Beef or Totem Pole Hot Fudge Brownie can head to Duggan's Irish Pub on Woodward north of 13 Mile, where owner Larry Payne has acquired the rights to the Totem Pole menu.

1960

FOR MANY YEARS IT WAS CUSTOMARY FOR THE DEMOCRATIC PRESIDENTIAL candidate to kick off his campaign with a Labor Day rally in Detroit. It made sense: With its heavy concentration of union members, ethnic voters and others who traditionally voted Democratic, the city was a bedrock of support. And with summer at its unofficial close, people were ready to concentrate on politics. Forty-four years ago, the handsome young senator from Massachusetts, John Fitzgerald Kennedy, exuding wit, smarts and a hopeful vision, won over the crowd assembled in downtown Detroit in an area that would one day be named after him — Kennedy Square. There were those who objected to Kennedy's Catholicism and others who equated his youth with inexperience. Conservative Republicans content with eight years of Eisenhower's leadership wanted to maintain the status quo with the current vice president, Republican candidate Richard Nixon. Still, in a real squeaker in November, Kennedy went on to defeat Nixon, becoming the 35th president of the United States and, at 43, its youngest elected president.

1960

GOLF GIANTS SAM SNEAD, ARNOLD PALMER, WALTER HAGEN AND GENE Sarazen have all teed off at Redford's Western Golf & Country Club. But some mighty big musical figures have performed there, too, including trumpeter Louis Armstrong, who's seen here transfixing guests at a party after the Western Open of 1960. Designed in 1926 by renowned Scottish golf architect Donald Ross (who also crafted Oakland Hills Country Club in Bloomfield Township), Western boasts a park-like setting that includes well-placed bunkers, doglegs and ponds, as well as the Rouge River meandering through it. Western also offers swimming, tennis and dining facilities.

1962

THE HUDSON'S THANKSGIVING DAY PARADE ON WOODWARD WAS AS TRADItional as pumpkin pie and turkey. At the end of the procession, the bulky man in red disembarked at Hudson's, signaling the official start of the Christmas shopping season. Back in the early '60s, live children's shows in Detroit were hugely popular, evidenced by this quintet of kids' heroes riding on a float: from left, Milky the Clown, Bwana Don, Bozo the Clown, Ricky the Clown and Sagebrush Shorty. Although the parade, now called America's Thanksgiving Parade, is still functioning, it just isn't the same without Hudson's, which was imploded in October of 1998.

1962

IN THESE DAYS OF COMFY, ENCLOSED SPORTS STADIUMS, IT'S HARD TO IMAGine that, not so many years ago, most pro football teams battled in the elements, turning the turf — and their uniforms — into a muddy mess. Long a Thanksgiving Day tradition, the Lions games at Tiger Stadium attracted a hardy crowd who bundled up, squirreled away a Thermos of hot coffee or perhaps a flask of whiskey, and braved brisk winds, cold rain or even snow. The Green Bay Packers were the Lions' great rivals, whom they played on Thanksgiving from 1951 through 1963. In 1962, the Packers, with the aid of flashy quarterback Bart Starr, were favored to trounce the Lions. In this photo, Starr is halted by tough Lions linemen, including Darris McCord and Roger Brown. The Lions went on to pull an upset over the Packers, 26-14, making Thanksgiving dinner all that much sweeter for Lions fans.

1963

DURING A DECADE OF SEISMIC SOCIAL UNREST AND VIOLENCE, BAPTIST minister and activist Martin Luther King Jr. stood out in the '60s as a staunch proponent of civil rights through peaceful means. On June 23, 1963, King (seen here waving) led a group of 125,000 down Woodward in an orderly demonstration for racial equality. King's gifts as a silver-tongued orator were in evidence that June day as he delivered a preview of the famous "I Have a Dream" speech — two months before that oft-quoted address was made to a quarter-million people during the March on Washington. King visited the Detroit area again in March of 1968, when he appeared at Grosse Pointe South High School. A few weeks later, on April 4, he was assassinated in Memphis, Tenn., where he had come to support striking sanitation workers.

⸎

1963 One of the Detroit area's most enduring symbols of its automotive might is the giant Uniroyal tire on I-94 in Allen Park. Before it became a Detroit landmark, it served as a Ferris wheel at the 1964 New York World's Fair. Jacqueline Kennedy and her children, Caroline and John Jr., even took a whirl on the mammoth eight-story ride. After the fair, the tire was moved to Michigan, where it was rebuilt — the Ferris wheel assembly being replaced by a supporting steel structure. In 1994, it received a face-lift, complete with a shiny new hubcap. The tire was deliberately jabbed with a 500-pound nail in 1998, in a publicity feat to promote the sturdy Uniroyal Tiger Paw NailGard. And wouldn't you know it, the world's largest tire didn't go flat.

1964

To children all over the city of Detroit, lazy summer days were always made more eventful by a visit from the Twin Pines milkman, the Awrey Bakery deliveryman, the Mr. Softee ice-cream vendor or the Bookmobile. Run by the Detroit Public Library (DPL), the Bookmobile was a lending library on wheels, especially appealing to kids or seniors unable to make it to their branch. In this photo from July 1964, kids line up to return books and no doubt check out new ones. Begun in 1940, Bookmobile service was, in a very real sense, an educational mission. Neighborhoods and schools with limited library services were targeted, as well as senior centers. Budget cuts put the brakes on the Bookmobile in 1992, but in 2000 voters approved a millage for expanded library services, and the Bookmobile was up and running again by the summer of 2002. Michael Wells, coordinator for specialized service at the DPL's Frederick Douglass branch, at Trumbull and Grand River, says two 28-foot custom-outfitted Bookmobiles serve elementary schools, senior housing and recreation centers. But the new versions are different in one way that these kids from 40 years ago could hardly imagine. In addition to books, Wells says each Bookmobile is capped by a satellite dish and contains computers equipped for Internet access.

1964

SCREAMS OF INEFFABLE JOY RANG OUT WHEN THE BEATLES PERFORMED IN early September at Detroit's Olympia Stadium on Grand River and McGraw. Tickets were an unbelievable $5, which were snapped up in no time. Hysteria is an understatement to describe the fervor the four lads from Liverpool incited wherever they went. As the premier battalion in the British Invasion, the Beatles generated a craze around the globe, aptly termed "Beatlemania." Even those who purported to despise rock 'n' roll pricked up their ears at the group's inventive melodies. In this shot, the Olympia audience goes ape as an unidentified Beatle waves to the crowd on his way to the stage. The Beatles would return to Detroit in 1966, again at Olympia. Later that year, at San Francisco's Candlestick Park, the group performed its last public concert, and to the consternation of millions, they broke up in 1970. Olympia is gone, too, but Beatlemania — even after the deaths of John Lennon and George Harrison — never has been entirely snuffed out.

1966 To generations of Detroiters, it just wasn't summer without a trip to Bob-Lo. Passengers boarding the steamers *Columbia* or *Ste. Claire* often were greeted by the diminutive Captain Bob-Lo, whose real name, appropriately, was Joe Short. The boats plied the waters of the Detroit River, taking visitors to the Canadian island for a leisurely day of picnicking or catching a thrill on Bob-Lo's many amusement park rides, such as the Jet Ride, pictured here. French settlers christened the island Bois Blanc ("white woods") because of its numerous stands of white poplars and birches. It's thought that "Bob-Lo" resulted from an American butchering of the French name. In the first half of the 20th century, visitors enjoyed picnics or dancing at the spacious hall, designed by Albert Kahn. It wasn't until 1949 that Bob-Lo became an amusement park. "Moonlight Cruises" were another attraction. Under starry skies, passengers — many of them young sweethearts — cruised the river and danced to a live band on the boat. The fun came to an end in the mid-'90s, when the steamers and rides were auctioned off. Today, the island is a residential community of single homes, townhouses and condominiums.

1967

FRANK SINATRA NEVER SANG A TRIBUTE SONG ABOUT DETROIT THE WAY HE did for Chicago and New York, but he easily could have. Detroit was Sinatra's kind of town. He loved the restaurants here (Excalibur, Giovanni's, Vince's and Roma Cafe), and he loved the fans even more. Starry-eyed bobby-soxers turned out in droves for Sinatra in the 1940s at downtown's United Artists and Michigan theaters. The crowds never thinned throughout the years at the Fox, Joe Louis, Pine Knob or Cobo Arena, where these photos were shot. Even when his whiskey-soaked voice had lost some of its flexibility, there was that unparalleled phrasing, the tender vulnerability he communicated in a ballad, the breezy swing of his upbeat tunes that could lift the most downtrodden soul. Frankie's pipes are silent now, but the very good years he gave Detroit will resonate for a long, long time.

1967

IN AN ERA OF HIPPIES, DOPE AND GUITAR ARMIES, SAN FRANCISCO HAD Haight-Ashbury, and Detroit had Plum Street — a collection of boutiques, coffee shops, antique stores and pottery shops. The enclave, on the western fringe of downtown Detroit, was intended to be Detroit's arts community — and for a brief time it was. The area had the city's official blessing, with Detroit Mayor Jerry Cavanagh and Gov. George Romney attending the grand opening in 1966. Merchants painted their storefronts in neon-hued psychedelic colors, and the neighborhood attracted scores of hippies, who in turn drew flocks of decidedly un-hip curiosity-seekers. But they all soaked up the bohemian atmosphere, which included such businesses as The Body Shop, Of Cabbages and Kings, Tres Camp, Above It All, Red Roach Coffee Shop, Joint Venture, The Plum Street Pottery Shop, Oddity Earring Shop and the Hai-Ku Coffee Shop. To add to the ambience, art exhibits and blaring rock 'n' roll concerts filled a nearby park. In this photo, taken at Plum and Fourth, tourists in the forefront blended in with youth (center). Tiger Stadium looms in the distance. The 1967 riot drove some businesses and visitors away, and motorcycle gangs scared off the remaining tenants. The area was leveled eventually and, like the Summer of Love, remains a dim memory.

1968

SOME 2,700 PEOPLE PACKED THE AUDITORIUM ON MARCH 14, 1968, AT Grosse Pointe South High School to listen to Dr. Martin Luther King Jr. speak on "The Future of Segregation." King was interrupted repeatedly by the heckling and insults of Donald Lobsinger, leader of the ultra-right group Breakthrough, and his followers. Outside, about 200 demonstrators picketed with signs declaring, "Christ is King, Not Vice Versa." However, the protest failed to discourage King. He announced to the crowd that it had inspired the theme for his upcoming Lenten service: "Forgive them, for they know not what they do." Exactly three weeks later, on April 4, 1968, the civil rights leader was assassinated in Memphis.

1968 WHEN THE UNDERDOG DETROIT TIGERS BEAT THE ST. LOUIS CARDINALS to win the World Series on the afternoon of Oct. 10, jubilant pandemonium spread quickly throughout metro Detroit. Streamers and confetti rained from downtown skyscrapers, a cacophony of car horns and noisemakers rang out, and major thoroughfares like Woodward and Jefferson were clogged with merrymakers. Downtown Detroit looked like the scene of a wild bacchanal, with ecstatic office workers taking to the streets and whooping it up, as this photo shows. The celebratory spirit was particularly intense, since only a year before the city had been torn asunder by a devastating riot. So when Bill Freehan, Gates Brown, Denny McLain, Mickey Lolich and their teammates led the Tigers to victory, they also contributed immeasurably in helping a city to heal its wounds.

1968

Robert Francis Kennedy, brother of the slain president and himself a Democratic candidate for president in 1968, is seen greeting well-wishers on Detroit's 12th Street (now Rosa Parks Boulevard) on May 15, 1968 — less than a year after that area was devastated by a violent riot that rocked the city. A month before this photo was taken, Martin Luther King Jr. was assassinated in Memphis. Although racial tensions were high, Sen. Kennedy, a staunch crusader for civil rights, was widely admired by black Americans and was enthusiastically welcomed whenever he appeared in predominantly African-American neighborhoods. While serving as attorney general under his brother, RFK — or "Bobby," as he was affectionately called — helped draft the Civil Rights Act, which was passed after the president died. It was under RFK's orders that black student James Meredith received federal protection as he enrolled at the University of Mississippi in 1962. Although he had definite foes, RFK's charisma and unwavering views drew strong support from black and white voters, and momentum gathered in his quest for the White House. But on June 5, 1968, he was shot by Sirhan B. Sirhan in a Los Angeles hotel after delivering a speech celebrating his California primary victory. He died the next day at age 42.

1976

DURING AMERICA'S BICENTENNIAL, CELEBRATIONS WERE COMMON — ESPEcially musical ones. Here, on Flag Day (June 14), the Detroit Symphony Orchestra performs a free afternoon concert in front of the old Hudson's building downtown as music lovers fill Woodward Avenue. At the time, Hudson's was a sponsor of the orchestra. On the podium is Detroit-born conductor Philip Greenberg. Although it can't be seen, the world's largest American flag, which adorned six stories of the Woodward side of Hudson's, was on display, as it was every Flag Day. The bicentennial was the last year that Hudson's unfurled the gargantuan flag; the department store donated it to the Smithsonian later that year.

1976 ARETHA FRANKLIN STILL REIGNS AS THE QUEEN OF SOUL, BUT HER EARLY efforts were in gospel music. She inherited that talent honestly, since she was the daughter of the famous Rev. C.L. Franklin, pastor of Detroit's New Bethel Baptist Church on Linwood. Rev. Franklin was a renowned gospel singer in his own right, and he toured with Aretha when she was a teen. Young Aretha sang regularly in the church, and when she was just 14 her powerful pipes were evident on the 1956 album *The Gospel Sound of Aretha Franklin*. Here, Franklin is photographed with young admirers outside the church at a press conference on March 26, 1976, a day after her 34th birthday. Although she's most famous for such soul classics as "Respect" and "Chain of Fools," Franklin returned to her gospel roots in the late '80s with the album *One Lord, One Faith, One Baptism*. Franklin's longevity is tied to her versatility, whether teaming up for a duet with George Michael or subbing for an indisposed Luciano Pavarotti at the 1998 Grammys with a memorable rendition of Puccini's "Nessun dorma."

1987 WHEN CARDINAL KAROL WOJTYLA BECAME THE FIRST POLISH POPE IN 1978, he didn't opt to be an aloof religious figurehead who holed up in Vatican City. Instead, Pope John Paul II traveled the globe, becoming a beloved figure even among some non-Catholics. On Sept. 18 and 19, 1987, the pope visited heavily Catholic metro Detroit, speaking at Blessed Sacrament Cathedral, celebrating Mass in the Pontiac Silverdome, addressing deacons in Ford Auditorium and appearing at Hart Plaza. But the most sentimental stop for many was Hamtramck, home to a legion of Polish-Americans. Residents lined the streets and waved Polish and American flags, along with signs exclaiming "Witamy!" — Polish for "Welcome!" In this shot taken in Hamtramck, two people in traditional Polish garb meet the smiling pontiff. A statue of the pope at Joseph Campau and Belmont is a lasting reminder of his connection to those of Polish extraction. Even today, the frail pope continues to travel.

Index

Index

Index